KAMISAKA SEKKA

RINPA TRADITIONALIST, MODERN DESIGNER

THE CLARK CENTER FOR JAPANESE ART AND CULTURE   ANDREAS MARKS

Pomegranate

SAN FRANCISCO

Published by Pomegranate Communications, Inc.
Box 808022, Petaluma CA 94975
800 227 1428 • www.pomegranate.com

Pomegranate Europe Ltd.
Unit 1, Heathcote Business Centre, Hurlbutt Road
Warwick, Warwickshire CV34 6TD, UK
[+44] 0 1926 430111 • sales@pomeurope.co.uk

Front cover: *Plum Tree (Ume)*. From *Things from Many Worlds*, vol. 2, 1909

Library of Congress Cataloging-in-Publication Data
Kamisaka, Sekka, 1866–1942.
 [Selections. English. 2012]
 Kamisaka Sekka : Rinpa traditionalist, modern designer / Andreas Marks.
   p. cm.
 Includes bibliographical references.
 ISBN 978-0-7649-6175-5 (hardcover)
 1. Kamisaka, Sekka, 1866–1942—Themes, motives. I. Marks, Andreas. II. Kamisaka, Sekka, 1866–1942. Cho senshu. III. Kamisaka, Sekka, 1866–1942. Momoyogusa. IV. Kamisaka, Sekka, 1866–1942. Chigusa. V. Title. VI. Title: Rinpa traditionalist, modern designer.
 NE1325.K25A4 2012
 769.92—dc23
                                      2011036979
Pomegranate Catalog No. A206

Designed by Stephanie Odeh

This book was printed in the USA using soy-based inks. The paper includes 10% post-consumer waste (PCW) recycled content. The paper is Forest Stewardship Council (FSC), Sustainable Forest Initiative (SFI), and Programme for the Endorsement of Forest Certification (PEFC) certified.

21 20 19 18 17 16 15 14 13 12   10 9 8 7 6 5 4 3 2 1

CONTENTS

KAMISAKA SEKKA

In 1868, under Emperor Meiji (1852–1912), the feudal rule of the Tokugawa shogunate over Japan collapsed and imperial power was reinstated. This brought to a close more than 250 years of relative isolation and opened the country to the West, initiating a rapid modernization and redefinition of Japan itself. Kamisaka Sekka (1866–1942) was born into this vibrant time and became an ardent follower of the decorative Rinpa painting tradition. Leading the revival of Rinpa in the early twentieth century, Sekka is sometimes referred to as the "Last Great Rinpa Artist." While apt, that title obscures his importance as a progenitor of modern design in Japan. Though deeply rooted in tradition, Sekka was a genius in creating imaginative, innovative designs and cooperating with other artists to apply them to lacquerware, textiles, ceramics, and furniture. In doing so he became an influential transitional figure, pioneering a consciousness of modern Japanese design and production.

The term "Rinpa," built from the syllable *rin* in Kōrin and the word *pa* (also *ha*) for "school," was coined in the Meiji period (1868–1912), but it describes a style created in the seventeenth century by Kyoto artists Tawaraya Sōtatsu (died c. 1643) and Hon'ami Kōetsu (1558–1637). Some earlier terms for this decorative painting tradition are still in use today, among them "Kōetsu school" (*Kōetsuha*) and "Sōtatsu Kōrin school" (*Sōtatsu-Kōrinha*).

The original Rinpa artists, Sōtatsu and Kōetsu, combined the decorative tradition of Yamato-e (Japanese-style images originating in the Heian period, 794–1185) with stylistic influences from subsequent periods. The two rendered themes like flowers, trees, animals, landscapes, and classical literary tales in bold compositions and vibrant colors. The subsequent generation of Rinpa artists included brothers Ogata Kōrin (1658–1716), active in the late seventeenth and early

Opposite: "Ōshukubai" (Noh play), detail (p. 45)

eighteenth centuries, and Ogata Kenzan (1663–1743), active in the eighteenth century, who further developed the style to include abstract forms in complete disregard of realism and convention. They also made liberal use of precious materials like gold and mother-of-pearl in their works. In the first half of the nineteenth century came the third generation of Rinpa artists, most notably Sakai Hōitsu (1761–1821) and Suzuki Kiitsu (1796–1858). Born in Edo (today's Tokyo), these two artists continued to steer Rinpa away from the longstanding cultural traditions of Kyoto toward the unconventional tastes of the new capital.

Instead of working exclusively in one medium like most artists of the time, Rinpa artists not only created paintings in various formats but also worked with artisans to decorate ceramics, lacquerware, and textiles. In addition, they often purposely covered the same subjects as their Rinpa predecessors, effectively creating an intergenerational series of works, each with its own distinctive identity and appeal. For example, inspired by Sōtatsu's *Wind and Thunder Gods* (*Fūjin Raijin zu*)—a pair of two-panel folding screens at Kyoto's Kennin-ji Temple—Kōrin composed his own version of the subject (now in the Tokyo National Museum), and Hōitsu, in turn, created his (in the Idemitsu Museum of Arts, Tokyo). Hōitsu included the screens in the 1826 reissue of his book *One Hundred Works by Kōrin* (*Kōrin hyakuzu*).

Sekka was born in Kyoto in 1866, the first of six sons of a samurai employed at the Imperial Palace. At the age of fif-teen he began to study the realistic painting techniques of the Shijō school under Suzuki Zuigen (1847–1901). In 1887 he researched textile design sketches at Kawashima textile factory and also studied European decorative arts under Shinagawa Yajirō (1843–1900), who had lived in Europe as a diplomat for the new Meiji government. Sekka soon turned toward Rinpa and began to study under Kishi Kōkei (1840–1922), an important early designer who later became an instructor at Kyoto Municipal School of Art.

In April 1890, at age twenty-four, Sekka started submitting artworks to expositions and competitions. That November, his *People on the Street* (*Gaitō fūretsu*) took second prize honorable mention at the Japan Art Association exhibition. In the following years he entered on average three competitions per year, and in 1894 he served as design judge for an exhibition of the Kyoto Art Association, which he had joined the year before. That same year, Sekka married Onomura Tei (1878–1945). They would have four children. Yoshiaki, their first son, was born in 1895, followed by daughter Kiyo in 1901, son Saburō in 1903, and daughter Shizu in 1913.

Sekka was open to new ideas and influences and was active as an editor and teacher. In 1897, while serving as executive secretary of the Gonikai Kyoto Design Club, he began editing the club's journal *New Designs* (*Shinzuan*). In 1898 he became editor of *Kyoto Art Association Journal* (*Kyōto Bijutsu Kyōkai Zasshi*)—later renamed *Kyoto Art* (*Kyōto Bijutsu*)—a position he held until 1918. In May 1900 he became a technician for the Department of Design Regulation affiliated with the Kyoto Municipal School of Arts and Crafts, which is today the well-respected Kyoto City University of Arts (Kyōto-shiritsu Geijutsu Daigaku, or Kyōto Geidai). There he rose through the ranks, advancing to the position of instructor in 1903 and serving as a regular faculty member from October 1905 until his resignation in 1925.

In 1900, Sekka's early studies in European decorative art started to bear fruit. His first international success came at that year's Exposition Universelle, the Paris world's fair. There his *Design for Brocade Tablecloth* was accepted to be shown, and he won a gold medal for *Writing Cabinet with Spring and Autumn maki-e Designs,* which Kishi Kōkei and Sekka had designed for the Kyōto Shōbikai organization. Consequently, Kyōto Shōbikai commissioned Sekka to produce sketches for cabinets of *maki-e* (lacquer designs dusted with gold or other metal powder) that were prepared for the British royal palace. In 1901 he traveled to Europe for five months to observe the Glasgow International Exhibition (May 2–November 9, 1901) and to study European crafts design. On his return trip to Japan, Sekka was inspired by the sea voyage and produced a collection of wave patterns. In 1902 Unsōdō published this collection under the English title *Kairo: One Hundred Patterns of Waves by Sekka Kamisaka.* (The Japanese title is *Senshoku zuan: Kairo,* or *Textile Designs: The Sea Route;* see fig. 1.)

Fig. 1. Kamisaka Sekka. From *Textile Designs: The Sea Route,* 1902
Polychrome woodblock print, 36.8 x 25.3 cm
Clark Center for Japanese Art and Culture (1997.018)

Sekka continued to participate in world's fairs, as both exhibitor and judge. In 1904 he submitted his *Four Designs of Flowers and Grasses* to the 1904 Louisiana Purchase Exposition in St. Louis, Missouri; in 1915 he served as a judge for the Panama-Pacific International Exposition in San Francisco; and in 1921 he helped jury the France-Japan Exchange Art Exhibition in France. For Sekka's ongoing contribution to the latter exhibition, France twice decorated him (in 1926 and 1937) with the Royal Order of Cambodia (*Ordre Royal du Cambodge*). The Japanese government had previously bestowed upon him the decorations of seventh court rank, lower level (*jushichii*), in 1912; seventh court rank, upper level (*shōshichii*), in 1918; and sixth court rank, lower level (*jurokui*), in 1922.

All the while, Sekka continued to be an active and influential member of the local Kyoto art world, participating in numerous art associations and organizations. In 1907, for example, he founded the Kabikai, an arts and crafts research group focusing on creation of new works for the industrialized age.

Sekka's most productive period came in the early years of the twentieth century, when almost all of his books were issued. After the books, he continued with designs for interiors, showing again his skillful Rinpa technique. He found success as a painter furnishing aristocratic families, particularly those in Kyoto, with paintings in traditional Rinpa style reminiscent of past glory. Furthermore, he received numerous commissions from members of the Imperial family, even from the immediate family of the emperor. In 1913, for example, he prepared designs for

Fig. 2: Kamisaka Sekka. *Kusunoki Masashige Preparing for the Battle at Minato River*, around 1918. Hanging scroll. Ink and colors on paper, 129.1 × 52.2 cm. Clark Center for Japanese Art and Culture (1997.007)

the interior of the train used for the enthronement ceremony of Emperor Taishō (1879–1926), and in 1919, Empress Teimei (1884–1951) requested a writing desk and layered calligraphy box to celebrate the investiture of Crown Prince Hirohito (later Emperor Shōwa, 1901–1989).

The Westernization of Japan in the Meiji period brought a change to the traditional Japanese perception of art. New general terms appeared in order to categorize the arts, often reflecting Western hierarchies. Paintings were split into two categories: Yōga (Western painting) and Nihonga (Japanese painting). Recognized by the official art establishment in the 1890s, Yōga was art created with Western materials and techniques, following Western traditions. Nihonga, by contrast, was meant to propagate traditional Japanese aesthetics by drawing from established materials and motifs.

In 1907, the first Ministry of Education Art Exhibition (*Monbushō bijutsu tenrankai*), better known as the Bunten, supported this separation of the arts by recognizing only three submission categories: Nihonga, Yōga, and sculpture. In 1919 the Bunten evolved into the Teiten (*Teikoku Bijutsuin tenrankai*, or Exhibition of the Imperial Academy of Fine Arts), but submissions remained limited to the same three categories. Not until 1927 were print and crafts categories added.

This strict separation was not without criticism. Some artists, including Sekka, pointed out the considerable stylistic differences existing within the Nihonga category itself. In a 1919 article Sekka clearly stated that too many of the works considered Nihonga were actually derived from Chinese models, and that for him, the only "genuine Nihonga" (*junsui na Nihonga*) was Rinpa, especially that by Kōrin.[1]

Sekka continued to submit artworks to competitions and to exhibit his works until the age of seventy. In 1938 he retired to Sagano on the outskirts of Kyoto. He died there on January 4, 1942, at age seventy-five, shortly after the beginning of the Pacific War.[2] ❖

NOTES

1. Kamisaka Sekka, "Shumi no kakumeisha to shite no Kōrin," *Geien* 1, no. 6 (1919)

2. His age at death is sometimes given as 76 or 77. See, e.g., Jitsuko Ogura, "Biographical Timeline of Kamisaka Sekka (1866-1942)," in Wood and Ikeda, *Kamisaka Sekka,* p. 323, erroneously counting his age at birth as one and overlooking that he was born in February but passed away in January.

KAMISAKA SEKKA

AND THE PUBLISHER UNSŌDŌ

Rinpa was not an established, professional painting school; rather, artists associated themselves with the style through copying its earlier masters. Woodblock-printed books illustrating Rinpa paintings, especially those of Kōrin, helped propagate the style. (Kōrin himself never worked in book illustration, so books of his images were all produced posthumously.)[1] One such book is the *Kōrin Picture Album* (*Kōrin gafu*) from 1802 in two volumes with a total of twenty-five illustrations in light colors (fig. 3). It presents figure studies, flowers, and landscapes by the Rinpa-style painter Nakamura Hōchū (died 1819), who based the works on Kōrin's paintings. Hōchū was from Osaka. He came to Edo in the fall of 1801 and presumably stayed until early 1803. During that time he worked on *Kōrin Picture Album,* which was published by Ōmiya Yohei in late 1802.

The method of printing text with woodblocks came to Japan from China; the oldest surviving examples are ritual Buddhist texts from the eighth century. In Japan the printing industry grew steadily. An estimated two thousand publishers of books and single-sheet prints were active at different times during the Edo period (1603–1868).[2] The beginning of the print phenomenon, today better known as *ukiyo-e,* or "pictures of the floating world," dates to the second half of the seventeenth century. Early print artists were trained as painters and engaged in book illustrations before designing black-and-white prints intended to stand independently. In the 1740s, pioneering attempts were made to produce single-color prints, and by the mid-1760s multicolor printing was developed and was rapidly commercialized.

These commercial prints—featuring kabuki actors, beauties, landscapes, and other motifs—became popular in the late eighteenth century and grew in popularity during the nineteenth century. Kitagawa Utamaro (1753–1806), Suzuki Harunobu (1725–1770), Katsushika Hokusai (1760–1849), and

Fig. 3. Nakamura Hōchū. Beach Plovers. From *Kōrin Picture Album,* vol. 2, 1802. Polychrome woodblock print, 25.8 x 37 cm. Clark Center for Japanese Art and Culture (1997.028)

Utagawa Hiroshige (1797–1858) were among the best-known ukiyo-e print designers. Just as painters of the time were doing, they moved away from strict Japanese artistic traditions and adopted a more realistic drawing style influenced by Western conventions. In the early 1870s newspapers became popular and gradually usurped some of the audience for ukiyo-e prints. During the last decades of the nineteenth century, demand for mass-produced art prints dropped, and the number of print designers and publishers declined greatly.

Sekka's first printed works were published in 1890 by Tanaka Jihei and his firm Bunkyūdō. *Different Tastes in Kyoto Dyework: Vestiges of the Old Capital (Bekkō kyōzome: Miyako no omokage)* consists of fifty-four images that fall under the category of clothing design. Bunkyūdō was established in Kyoto around 1869, and by 1901, when the firm moved to Tokyo, it had published two more books by Sekka, as well as the Sekka-edited journal *New Designs by Gonikai.*

The firm Unsōdō, which still exists today, became Sekka's primary publisher. It was founded in 1891 by Yamada Naosaburō, who had previously worked for Bunkyūdō. Among the first books Unsōdō produced was *The Essence Book (Seikajō)*, published in 1892. It reproduced twenty images, each by a different painter from the recent past, including Yokoyama Seiki (1792–1864). Unsōdō also commissioned popular living painters such as Takeuchi Seihō (1864–1942) and reproduced their paintings in print; for example, *Twelve Mt. Fuji by Seihō (Seihō jūni Fuji)* from 1894. Finally, the firm became a major publisher of pattern and design books for artisans and manufacturers of lacquerware, ceramics, textiles, metalwork, and other products.

Pattern books had been known in Japan since the seventeenth century. *A New Selection of Respected Patterns (Shinsen on-hiinagata)* from 1666, offering seventy-seven different kimono designs drawn by an unknown artist, is considered the earliest of this type. Among Unsōdō's early offerings were *New Designs for the Decorative Arts (Kōgei shinzu)* by Tanaka Yūhō (dates unknown), published in 1892, and *Handbook of Art Patterns (Moyō bijutsu benran)* by Asai Hironobu (dates unknown), from the following year. Until the mid-1930s, Unsōdō collaborated with important figures in Japan's design scene—including Furuya Kōrin (1875–1910) and Mori Yūzan (died 1917)—while establishing a reputation as the foremost publisher of design books in Japan. In terms of quantity and diversity, the peak for such books was around the turn of the twentieth century.

Unsōdō began to publish Sekka's creations in 1899 with the collection *All Kinds of Things (Chigusa)*. By the time *Poem Pictures (Uta-e)* was published in 1934, Unsōdō had produced a total of eleven books with Sekka as sole author or contributor. Among them are *All Kinds of Butterflies (Chō senshu)* and *Things from Many Worlds (Momoyogusa)*, Sekka's best-known works, which Unsōdō has reproduced several times since. The Imperial Japanese Commission selected some of Unsōdō's publications, including *All Kinds of Things, Textile Designs: The Sea Route,* and *Humorous Designs* (*Kokkei zuan;* fig. 4), for the Louisiana Purchase Exposition in 1904.[3]

Textile Designs: The Sea Route and *All Kinds of Butterflies* are typical pattern books presenting a wide range of possibilities around one distinctive subject and for a specific purpose. Unsōdō published *The Sea Route* in August 1902, *Humorous Designs* in April 1903, and *All Kinds of Butterflies* one year later. Intended for textile design, *The Sea Route* features ninety-seven wave shapes and water patterns over thirty-five pages. Some of them are in organic forms; others bear geometric patterns, reflecting Sekka's exposure to a wide range of art styles during his journey to Europe.

Like *The Sea Route, Humorous Designs* also carries an English title in roman letters: *Kokkei Zuan, A Collection of Humorous Designs, by Sekka Kamisaka, the Author of "Kairo."* This indicates that both books were either meant for an international market or intended to convey an international flair appealing to Japanese buyers. *Humorous Designs* presents forty-six witty pictures on thirty pages. It is the only such book by Sekka where all pictures are accompanied by a short title, usually placed on their right. In the preface Sekka underlines that these pictures were conceived lightheartedly as an expression of his humor.

Sekka's images were transformed into dramatic woodcuts for the books, which, like all of those published by Unsōdō, were lavishly printed in limited editions of a very high standard of quality. Mass publication allowed Sekka's work to reach a

Fig. 4. Kamisaka Sekka. Beauty-flowers, from *Humorous Designs,* 1903
Polychrome woodblock print, 19 x 25.4 cm
Clark Center for Japanese Art and Culture (1997.016)

considerably larger audience than his original paintings were able to. However, he had to revise his style to adapt to the needs of the wood-carver while ensuring superior and powerful graphics. Yamazaki Yasutarō was Unsōdō's main printer between at least 1894 and 1903 and produced *Twelve Mt. Fuji by Seihō, All Kinds of Things,* and *Humorous Designs.* We unfortunately don't know much about him. In fact, other than their names, we know little about any of the craftsmen Unsōdō employed as carvers and printers. ❖

NOTES

1. For a list, see David G. Chibbett, *The History of Japanese Printing and Book Illustration* (Tokyo: Kodansha International, 1977), 206–7.

2. Hillier, *Japanese Book,* vol. 1, 28.

3. International Exposition, ed., *Empire of Japan: Official Catalogue* (St. Louis: International Exposition, 1904), 69.

❖ **All Kinds of Things** | Chigusa

❖ **All Kinds of Butterflies** | Chō senshu

❖ **Things from Many Worlds** | Momoyogusa

THREE ALBUMS; POLYCHROME WOODBLOCK PRINTS; PUBLISHED BY UNSŌDŌ, KYOTO

VOL. 1, September 1900 (Set 1–9, Feb. 1899–June 1900), 34 pages, 30 pictures, album and picture size 23.6 x 35.2 cm

VOL. 2, September 1901, 16 pages, 12 pictures, album and picture size 23.6 x 35.5 cm

VOL. 3, April 1903, 24 pages, 12 pictures, album and picture size 23.6 x 35.3 cm. Works in this volume are untitled.

The edition illustrated here is from April 1903, vols. 1 and 3, and June 1903, vol. 2.

The collection *All Kinds of Things* was originally not available in three bound albums as it is known today but was issued in sets of three pictures each. According to the colophon of the original edition at Chiba University Library, it was the intention to issue one set on the twenty-fifth of every month and to conclude the series with fifty sets, which would have meant 150 pictures (considerably more than the actual fifty-four existing pictures). A set was available for thirty *sen* plus two *sen* postage, and those who paid in advance for a ten-month subscription were offered these prints as a luxury-bound album.[1] It seems, however, that the production did not proceed as planned as the following list of publication dates shows:

SET 1: February 25, 1899	SET 4: June 25, 1899	SET 7: October 25, 1899
SET 2: April 25, 1899	SET 5: July 25, 1899	SET 8: January 25, 1900
SET 3: May 25, 1899	SET 6: January 25, 1900	SET 9: June 25, 1900

The tenth set was apparently never issued independently but only as part of the final first album. The first bound album with thirty pictures (or ten sets) as we know it today was then produced for the first time in September 1900. Remarkably, the order of appearance of the pictures in the sets and the bound volume differ in one instance: *Pampas Grasses (Obana)* (p. 35), the third picture of the fifth set, should have become the fifteenth picture of the bound album but is instead the eighteenth, preceded by the three pictures of set six.

After the first volume was issued in bound form, the publisher did not continue to produce monthly sets but issued two more bound volumes, each with twelve new pictures. Volume 2 appeared in September 1901, one year after the first volume, while Sekka was traveling in Europe. Volume 3 finally followed in April 1903. The first reprints of volumes 1 and 2 were issued in June 1903, and those of volume 3 were issued in February 1905.[2]

We cannot with certainty determine today in which way Sekka originally provided the pictures for *All Kinds of Things*. From a practical point of view it is unlikely that he designed increments of three pictures; it seems more likely that he created several, if not all, at once and then the publisher picked which pictures he would produce first. Considering the publication date of volume 2, Sekka obviously must have created its pictures before his departure to Europe at the end of July 1901.

Three woodblock carvers and five printers were originally commissioned for this project. Wada Tsuruzō, Matsuzaki Tetsutarō, and Tsukamoto Hirokichi were the carvers, and Yamanaka Izō, Ishitani Takematsu, Ichikawa Yasutarō, Tadokoro Rikimatsu, and Yamazaki Yasutarō were the printers, the latter producing more than half of the first edition and the reprints at least until 1903. Fujita Ryōgorō was the book binder for the entire first edition.

Chigusa literally translates as "a thousand grasses" (or herbs), and "thousand" also signifies "all kinds" or "innumerable." *All Kinds of Things* was clearly not created to serve as a pure pattern book but as a collection of beautiful images that could be appreciated as such. The first and second volumes are similar in motif and design, and both start with a table of contents identifying the pictures to follow. The subjects are taken from classical motifs (kimono, fans, picture scrolls) or from nature (birds, plants, famous landscapes). While some refer directly to literary themes or Noh plays such as *Takasago,* others bear literary associations. *Moonflower (Yūgao)* (p. 51), for example, alludes to a character from *The Tale of Genji.*

Sekka's love for and training in the Rinpa tradition is especially visible in the images of the first two volumes that depict themes from nature. For example, the water of *Willow and Cherry Blossoms (Yanagi sakura)* (p. 19) and *Kamo River (Kamogawa)* (p. 28) resembles so-called "Kōrin water" (*Kōrin mizu*), a characteristic feature of Ogata Kōrin's painting style.

The third volume is significantly different from the previous two as its proximity to a pattern collection is much more apparent. It consists solely of white flowers silhouetted against solid color blocks of varying geometrical shapes, one to five shapes per flower image. The third volume is also bound differently, with just one picture on the left side of a double-page spread instead of a picture on every page. The disparity between the first two volumes and the third can be explained by the nineteen months' time gap between the publication of volumes 2 and 3 and Unsōdō's rising interest in pattern books. Volume 3 was issued after the publication of the pattern book *The Sea Route* and simultaneously with *Humorous Designs* and marks a shift toward patterns that do not rely on classical imagery. It is followed by another pattern book, *All Kinds of Butterflies*. ❖

NOTES

1. The *sen* is a currency unit that is the original subdivision of the yen.
2. Higa Akiko, "Kamisaka Sekka's Design Collection," in Wood and Ikeda, *Kamisaka Sekka,* p. 307, follows the colophon and erroneously states that the entire *All Kinds of Things* was originally issued in monthly sets of three pictures each from February 1899 to June 1900. This determination also does not work out mathematically, as the fifty-four existing pictures would have made eighteen sets (months), so if the first set came out in February 1899, the last set would have had to come out in July 1900.

Suminoe Shore and Longevity Dance | Suminoe Ennenmai

Willow and Cherry Blossoms | Yanagi sakura

Snowy Plum under the Moonlight | Gekka no yuki ume

Panorama of Maple Trees | Kaede no keshiki

Doll Kimono | Hinakosode

Wave-Flowers | Nami no hana

Deutzias | U-no-hana

"Whose Sleeves?" | Tagasode

Beach Plovers | Iso chidori

Wisteria Garden | Fujitsubo

Kamo River | Kamogawa

Autumn Moon | Aki no tsuki

"Three Brush Traces" (Ono no Michikaze, Fujiwara no Yukinari, Fujiwara no Sukemasa) | Sanseki

Flower Basket | Hanakago

Cranes in a Bay | Ura tsuru

The Thirty-Six Immortal Poets | Rokkasen [sic]

Takao | Takao

Pampas Grasses | Obana

"Wind in the Pines" (Noh play) | Matsukaze

Chrysanthemums | Oki no kiku

Snowcaps | Yuki bōshi

"Takasago" (Noh play) | Takasago

"Okina" (Noh play) with Auspicious Diamond Pattern | Saiwaibishi Okina

Toy Mice | Nezumi ningyō

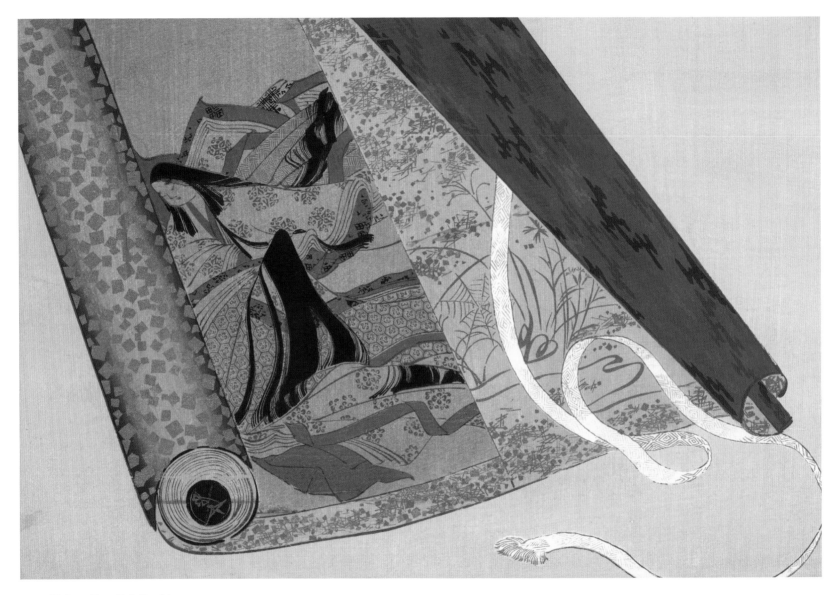

Picture Scroll | Emakimono

"Ōshukubai" (Noh play) | Ōshukubai

Fern | Shida

Round Fans | Uchiwa

Utsu Mountain | Utsu-no-yama

Autumn Flowers | Akigusa

First Sunrise of the New Year | Hatsu hinode

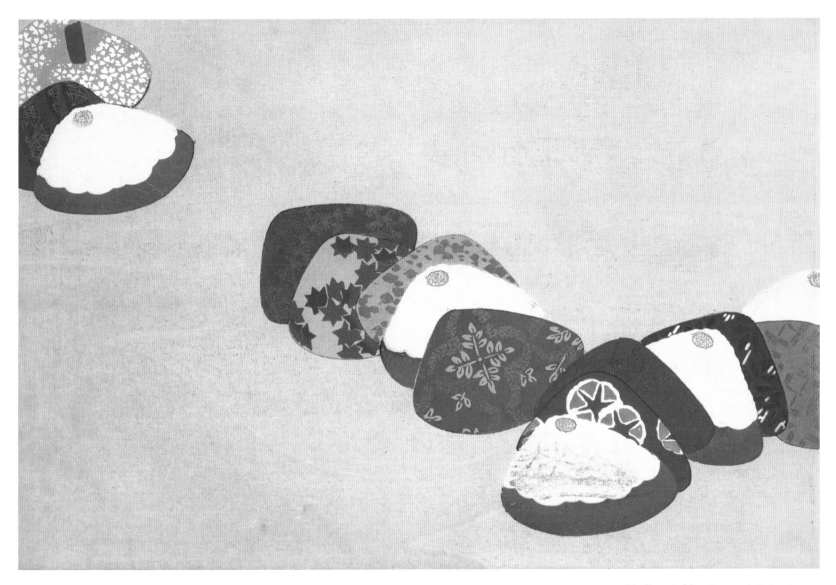

Shell-matching Game | Kai ooi

Decorated Colored Papers | Tsuya ashikishi

Moonflower | Yūgao

Kimono Curtain | Kosode maku

Incense Set | Takimono

Kimekomi Dolls | Kimekomi ningyō

Matsushima | Matsushima

Reeds and the Wheel of Law | Ashi hōrin

Autumn Road | Aki no machi

Pattern Books for Textile | Orimono chō

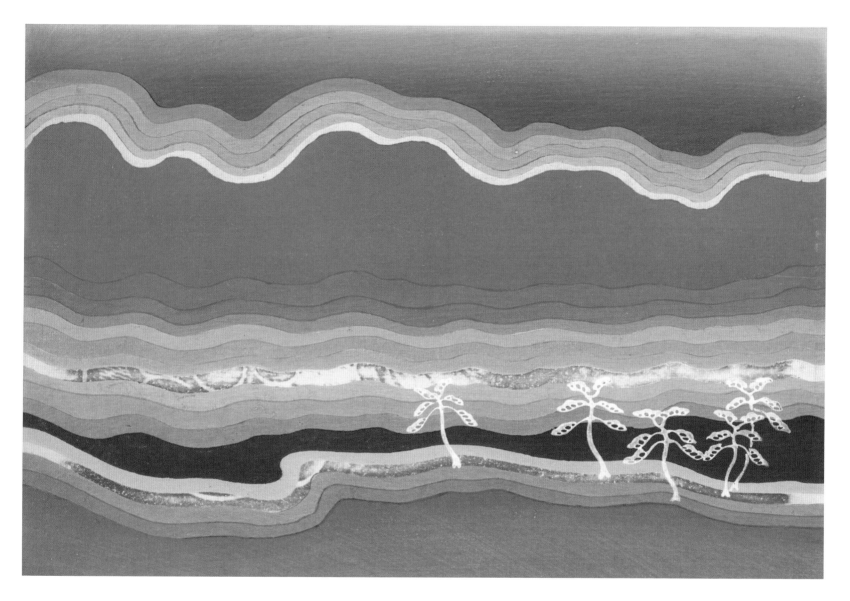

Pine Trees on the Seashore | Sonare no matsu

ALL KINDS OF BUTTERFLIES | Chō senshu

TWO ALBUMS, EACH FOLDED IN THE CENTER; POLYCHROME WOODBLOCK PRINTS;

PUBLISHED BY UNSŌDŌ, KYOTO

VOL. I, April 1904, 30 double pages, 25 pictures, album size 25 x 18 cm, picture size 25 x 35.9 cm

VOL. 2, October 1904, 27 double pages, 25 pictures, album size 25 x 18 cm, picture size 25 x 35.8 cm

The edition illustrated here is from February 1908. Works in these two albums are untitled.

Butterflies are an immensely popular motif in Japanese art. Their floating dance is seen to represent a sacred animal bringing the soul of the dead up to heaven. Moreover, the transformation of a butterfly from larva via pupa to a graceful creature was perceived as representing the rebirth of the soul. The butterfly became the symbol of longevity in Japan because *chō,* the word for "butterfly," is a homophone for the Chinese character for "long."

All Kinds of Butterflies consists of two volumes, each with twenty-five images of scattered butterflies.[1] In the first volume, the pictures of butterflies are preceded by a preface written by Ikebe (Konakamura) Yoshikata (1861–1923), who is considered one of the earliest scholars of National Literature (*kokubungaku*). In the preface, Ikebe retells a dream in which he saw colorfully dressed girls dancing and asking Sekka to paint them. Upon waking, he realized that the girls were butterflies, which is what Sekka painted.[2]

In *All Kinds of Butterflies* Sekka demonstrated his ingenious creativity as a designer by creating fifty different imaginary species of butterfly. Set against single-color backgrounds, the number of butterflies per image fluctuates from two to thirty-seven. Each image features just one type of butterfly. The butterfly species vary greatly in terms of shape, form, color, size, and pattern; some appear to be realistic depictions of an existing species, others are of more stylized design. Sekka's color combinations and choice of lines reveal the influence of Art Nouveau as well as the more traditional Rinpa style.

Most of the time the butterflies are shown motionless with their wings spread wide, but sometimes Sekka also explores motion and flight patterns, thus creating vivid impressions of movement. Sekka's butterflies offer a vast array of variations on a single theme and are intended for decorative purposes, particularly for textile makers. ❖

NOTES

1. Several different translations of the title exist. The Metropolitan Museum of Art published a facsimile edition of the first volume in 1979 under the title *A Flight of Butterflies* (see Kanzaka, *A Flight*). Hillier's *Japanese Book* and Wood and Ikeda's *Kamisaka Sekka* call it *A Thousand Butterflies,* while Keyes's *Ehon* calls it *One Thousand Butterflies.*
2. The preface is translated in part in Kanzaka, *A Flight*.

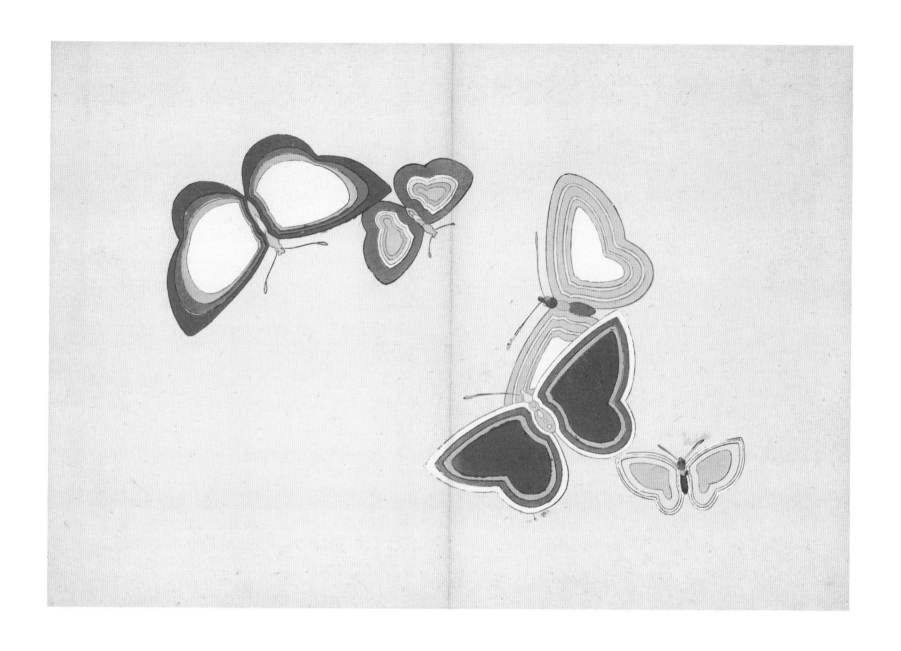

KAMISAKA SEKKA

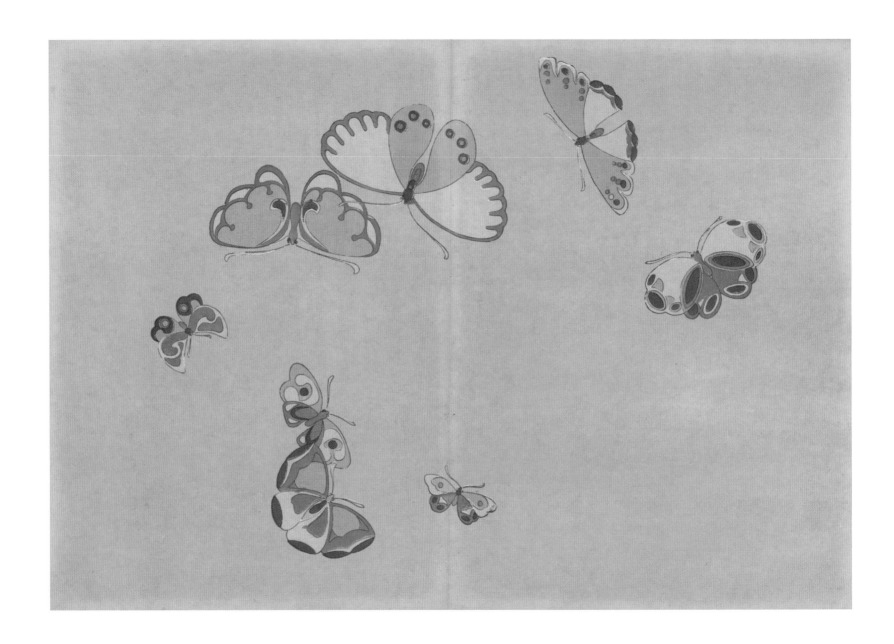

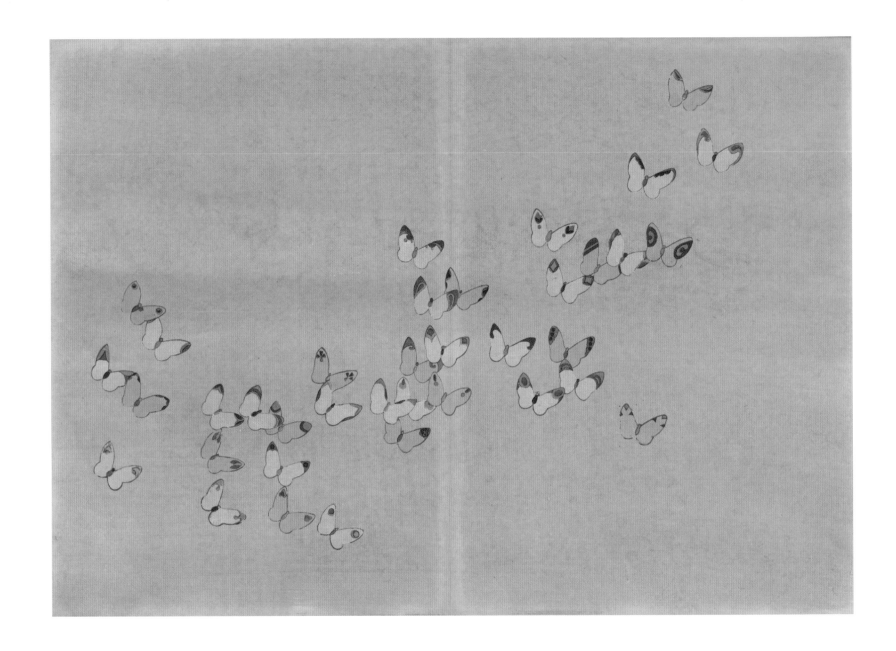

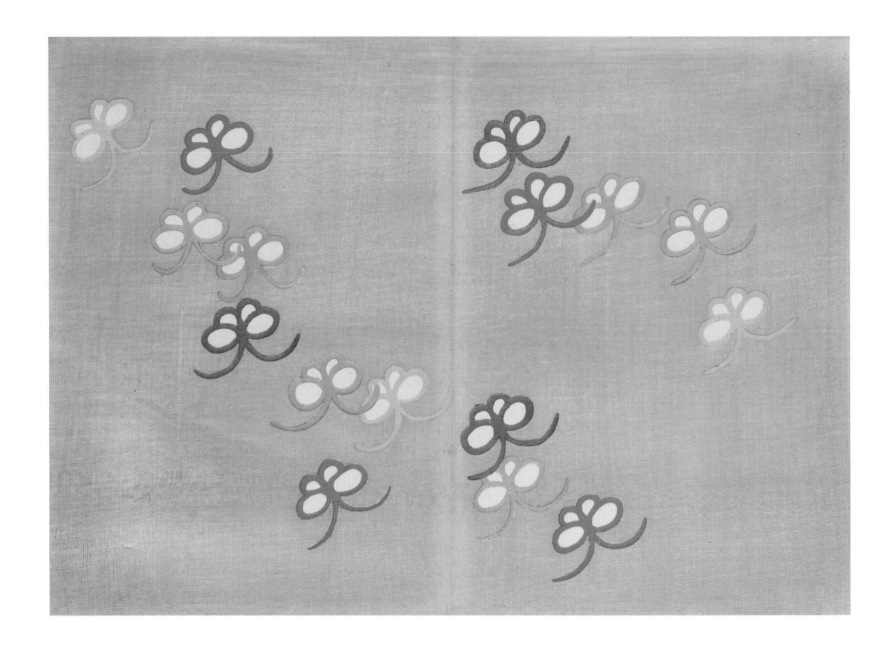

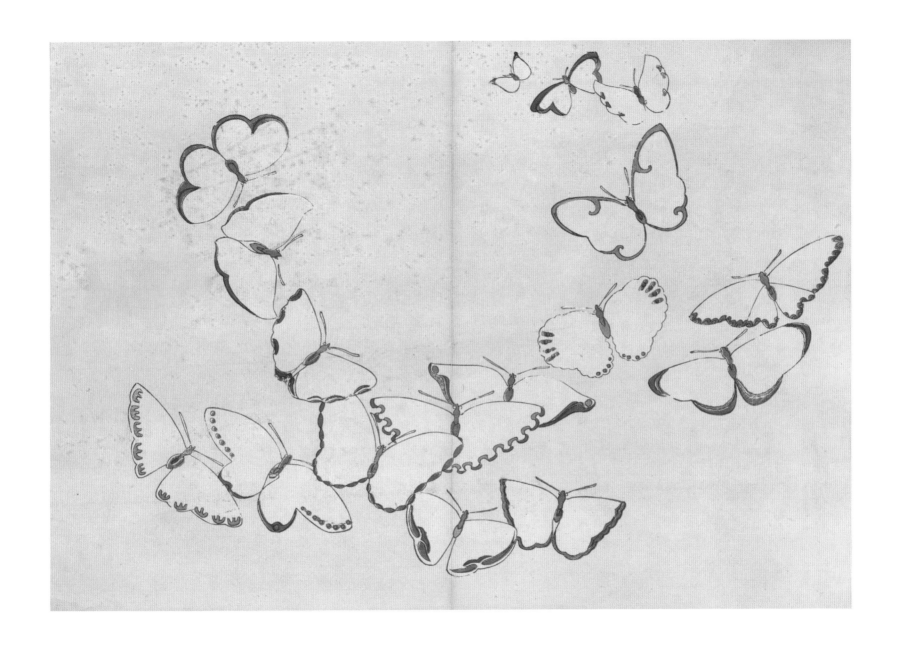

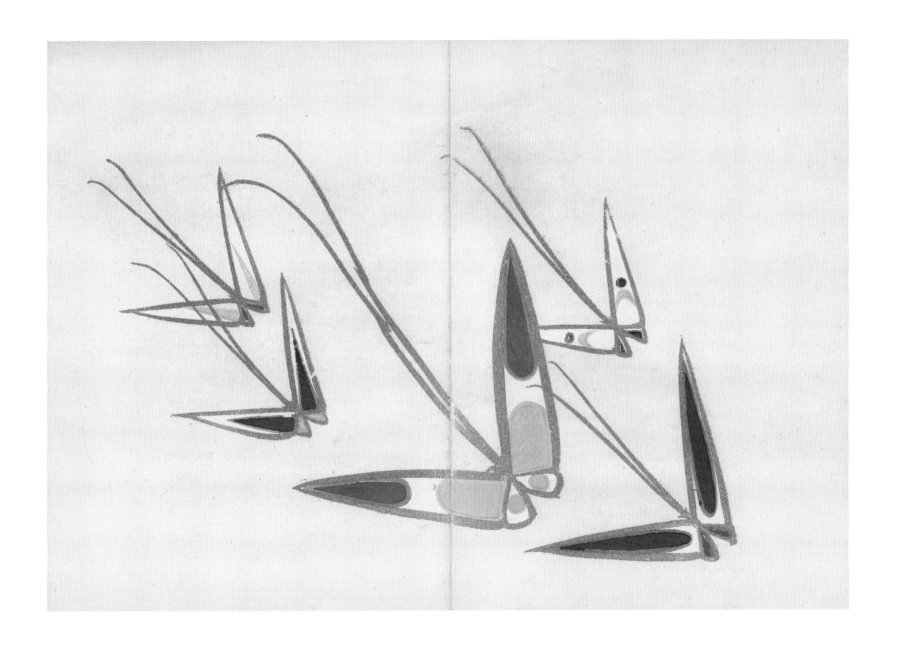

KAMISAKA SEKKA

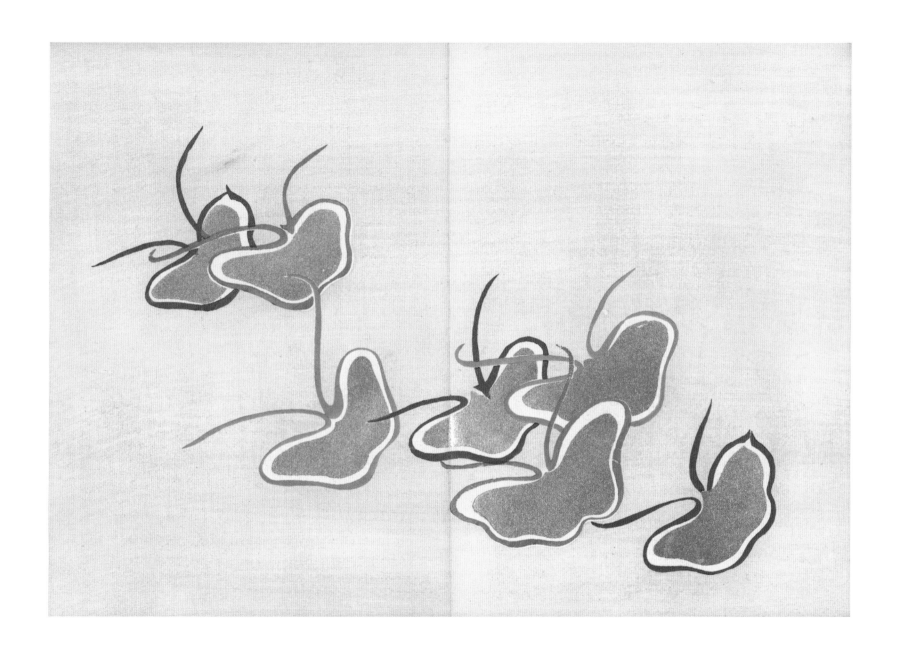

THREE ALBUMS, EACH FOLDED IN THE CENTER; POLYCHROME WOODBLOCK PRINTS; PUBLISHED BY UNSŌDŌ, KYOTO

VOL. I, May 1909, 24 double pages, 20 pictures, album size 30 x 22.3 cm, picture size 30 x 44.6 cm

VOL. 2, December 1909, 23 double pages, 20 pictures, album size 30 x 22.3 cm, picture size 30 x 44.5 cm

VOL. 3, January 1910, 23 double pages, 20 pictures, album size 30 x 22.2 cm, picture size 30 x 44.3 cm

This is the edition illustrated here.

Things from Many Worlds (*Momoyogusa*) is Sekka's undisputed masterwork, rich of jubilant and unconventional images of nature and traditional themes. The three folded albums were originally issued separately: the first in May 1909, the second in December of the same year, and the third the following January.[1] Each volume comprises twenty designs spread over double pages. The images are preceded by a table of contents identifying the images and, as in the previous books, succeeded by a colophon stating the date of printing, date of publication, and the names of artist and publisher. The first volume carries a double-page preface consisting of a poem by "Nobuyuki," who cannot be identified.[2]

Just how extraordinary and important this set is can be seen by the covers of each volume. The gray paper wrappers bear a silver wave design and a title slip with eccentric calligraphy by the famous painter Tomioka Tessai (1837–1924) (fig. 5). *Momoyogusa* is an autumnal herb that is a type of chrysanthemum. The individual characters mean "hundred ages herb," but "hundred"

Fig. 5. Title page from *Things from Many Worlds*, vol. I, 1909. Woodblock print, 30 x 22.3 cm. Clark Center for Japanese Art and Culture (1991.005)

(*momo*), like "thousand," also stands for "many" or "countless." It seems that Jack Hillier in 1987 was the first who offered the translation *Worlds of Things,* which was then altered to *A World of Things* by 1990.[3]

Like *All Kinds of Things, Things from Many Worlds* is intended as print art rather than as a collection of patterns. The sixty images display classical themes comparable to *All Kinds of Things,* but here Sekka presents them in a transformed, modernized Rinpa style. Common Rinpa motifs like plum blossoms and waves are brought to new life in sophisticated compositions with dazzling clarity and elegance. Bright and buoyant colors are applied in a bold, simple manner, creating a contemporary appeal that foreshadows the transition to modern design aesthetics. In *Thunder God (Kaminari)* (p. 168), for example, Sekka simplifies and demystifies the subject, transforming the inherently ferocious deity into a humorous one by capturing him with crossed eyes.

Although *Things from Many Worlds* is not a pattern collection per se, several of these pictures appear in Sekka's paintings and three-dimensional objects. The third picture in the third volume, *Autumn Night (Aki no yoru)* (p. 172), depicts a simple farmhouse behind reeds. A similar farmhouse appears again in some of his paintings and as decoration on the lids of black lacquer boxes. One of the closest resemblances is shown in figure 6; in other versions Sekka removed the window grate and shows a farmer in the house reading.[4]

A sharp-edged, snowcapped *Mt. Fuji* with a wavy peak is the thirteenth motif of the first volume (p. 142). Executed with just three colors, Japan's sacred mountain is set against a beige background and captured in white with a few simple brushstrokes in dark blue to indicate the uncovered rock. This composition with the same choice of color is seen in Sekka's paintings of Mt. Fuji, such as the fan-shaped work executed a few years later (fig. 6).[5]

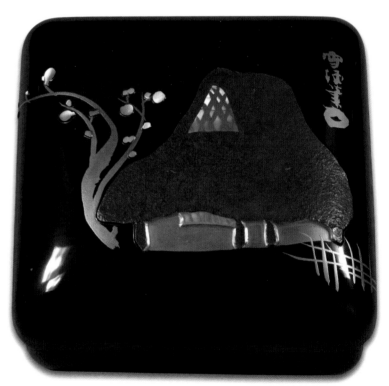

Fig. 6. Kamisaka Sekka. *Covered Box with Country House Designed by Sekka,* 1920–1930. Gold, lead, maki-e lacquer, and mother-of-pearl on wood, 5.3 x 11.7 x 11.7 cm. Clark Center for Japanese Art and Culture (1998.008)

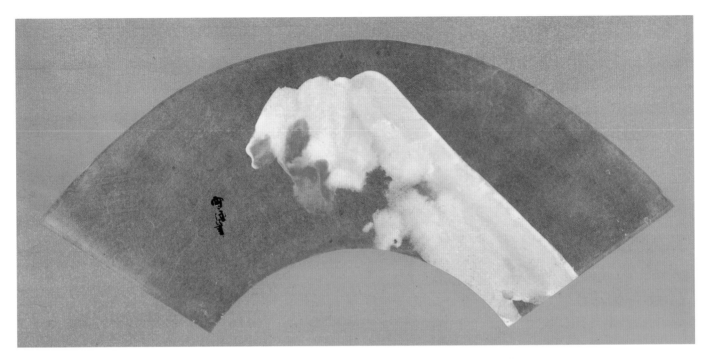

Fig. 7. Kamisaka Sekka. *Mt. Fuji,* 1920–1940. Hanging scroll. Ink, gold, and colors on paper, 16.4 x 51.2 cm. Clark Center for Japanese Art and Culture (1997.008)

As a final example, Sekka regularly painted pine trees using two distinctly different shapes that are also represented in *Things from Many Worlds. Meadow at Kasuga (Kasugano)* (p. 134) in volume 1 shows the straight type with upright trunk and pointed tip. The trees are arranged in an asymmetrical, parallel formation. The same composition is seen in figure 8, a folding fan where even the heights of the trees correspond with those in *Meadow at Kasuga. Pine Trees on the Seashore (Sonare no matsu)* (p. 182) in volume 3 illustrates the second type of pine tree with round crown bent to the

side and a thick stem ending in thin branches. Figure 9 shows a tray made of Paulownia wood with a painting by Sekka of such pine trees.

As indicated by the title, *Things from Many Worlds* brings aspects of many subjects to life, captivating the viewer with its outpouring of freshness, originality, and humor. It is an homage to Rinpa tradition and at the same time a modern and unique masterpiece that expresses Sekka's confidence and maturity as an artist. *Things from Many Worlds* is an important cornerstone for his legacy as the "Last Great Rinpa Artist." ❖

Fig. 8. Kamisaka Sekka. *Folding Fan with Pine Trees*, 1905–1915
Ink and colors on paper, 33 x 54.2 cm
Clark Center for Japanese Art and Culture (1997.011)

NOTES

1. These dates are identical in the colophons of the version at the Clark Center for Japanese Art and Culture, Hanford, CA (illustrated here), and of the version at the Art Gallery New South Wales, Sydney, Australia. The most recent reprint by Unsōdō erroneously gives February 1910 as the original publication date for the third volume; see Kamisaka and Higa, *Momoyogusa*, 5.

2. For a translation of the poem, see Keyes, *Ehon*, 240.

3. Hillier, *Japanese Book*, vol. 2, 975. Two entries for 1990 have been found: Helen Merritt, *Modern Japanese Woodblock Prints: The Early Years* (Honolulu: University of Hawai'i Press, 1990), 31; and The Year in Review: Selections 1989. In: *The Bulletin of the Cleveland Museum of Art* 77, no. 2 (1990): The translation *Flowers of a Hundred Worlds* is used in Keyes, *Ehon*, 240.

4. Wood and Ikeda, *Kamisaka Sekka*, figs. 155, 156-A.

5. For other examples, see Wood and Ikeda, *Kamisaka Sekka*, figs. 116–19.

Fig. 9. Kamisaka Sekka. *Tray with Old Pine Tree*, 1920–1940
Ink and colors on Paulownia wood and silver, 39.2 x 4 x 27 cm
Clark Center for Japanese Art and Culture (1997.022)

Flowers of a Hundred Worlds | Momoyogusa

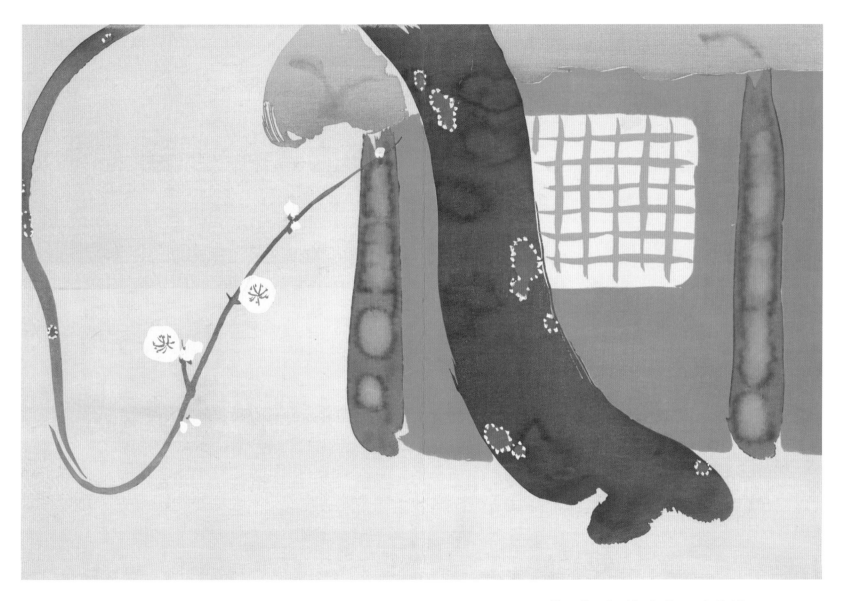

Plum Tree beside the Eaves | Nokiba no ume

Charcoal Seller | Kuroki uri

Fishing Village | Gyoson

Meadow at Kasuga | Kasugano

The Third Month | Yayoi

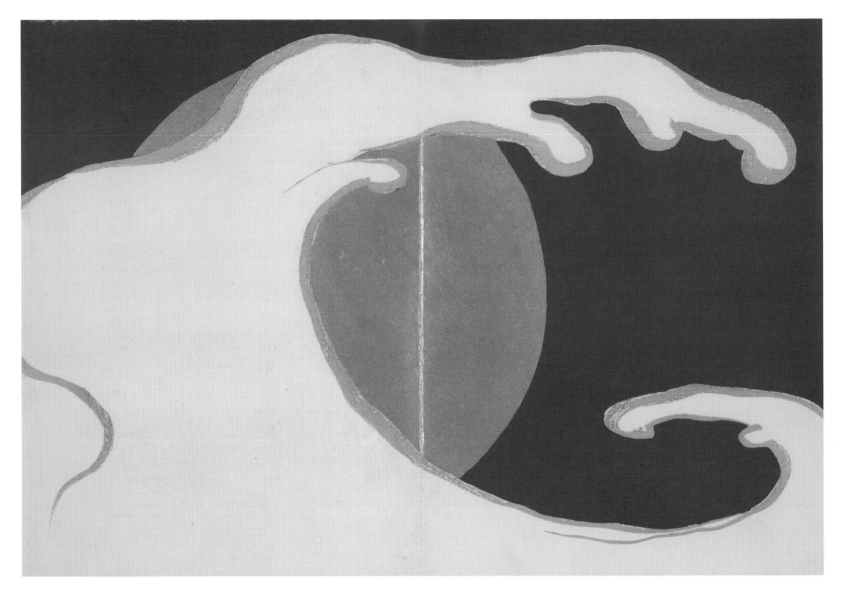

Cresting Wave | Tatsunami

Peonies | Fukamigusa

Eight Folded Bridge | Yatsuhashi

Ivy | Tsuta

Deutzias | U-no-hana

"Tadanori" (Noh play) | Tadanori

Mt. Fuji | Fuji

Folding Fans | Suehiro

Morning Glories | Asagao

White Phoenix | Hakuhō

Whirling Snow (Nichiren, 1222–1282) | Tomoe no yuki

"The Shrine in the Field" (Noh play) | Nonomiya

White Heron | Shirasagi

KAMISAKA SEKKA

Bamboo in Snow | Setchū no take

Ōtsu Folk Pictures | Ōtsu-e

Willow and Cherry Blossoms | Yanagi sakura

"Wait a Moment!" (Kabuki play) | Shibaraku

Woodcutter | Shōfu

"The Boat of Asazuma" (Kabuki play) | Asazuma-bune

Plum Tree | Ume

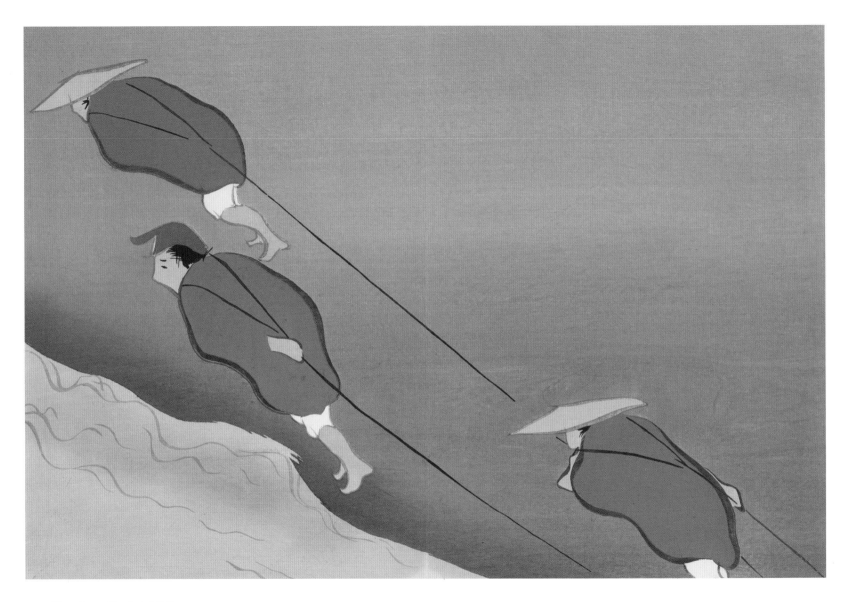

Tugging a Boat | Hikifune

Cranes | Tsuru

Pampas Grasses and the Moon | Obana ni tsuki

Imperial Guard | Eishi

"Chrysanthemum Boy" (Noh play) | Kikujidō

Cart with Flowers | Hanazashi-guruma

Hydrangea | Ajisai

Dancing | Odori

Bantams | Chabo

Wisterias | Fuji

Oxherd Boy | Bokudō

Puppies | Enokoro

Thunder God | Kaminari

Ripples | Sazanami

Rural Cottage in Spring | Haru no denka

Suminoe Shore | Suminoe

Autumn Night | Aki no yoru

Chinese Bellflowers | Kikukiri

Rice Paddies in Spring | Haru no tanomo

The Six Immortal Poets | Rokkasen

Dragon | Ryū

Late Spring | Boshun

Fulling Clothes | Tōi

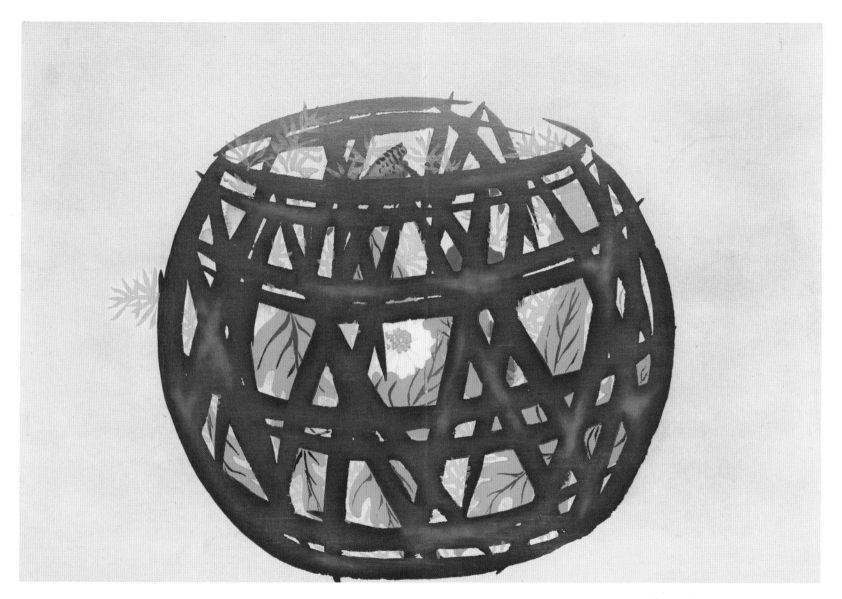

Flower Basket | Hanakago

The God Hotei | Hotei

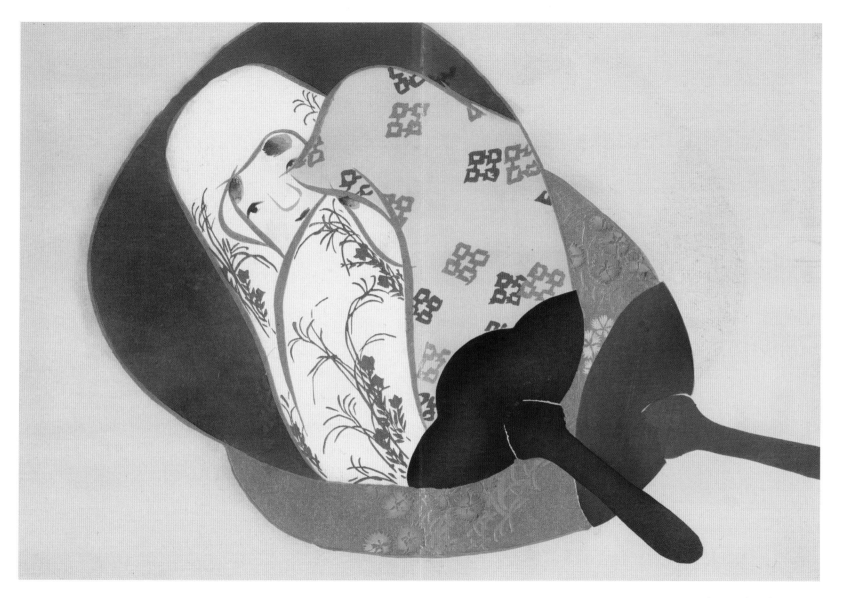

Round Fans | Uchiwa

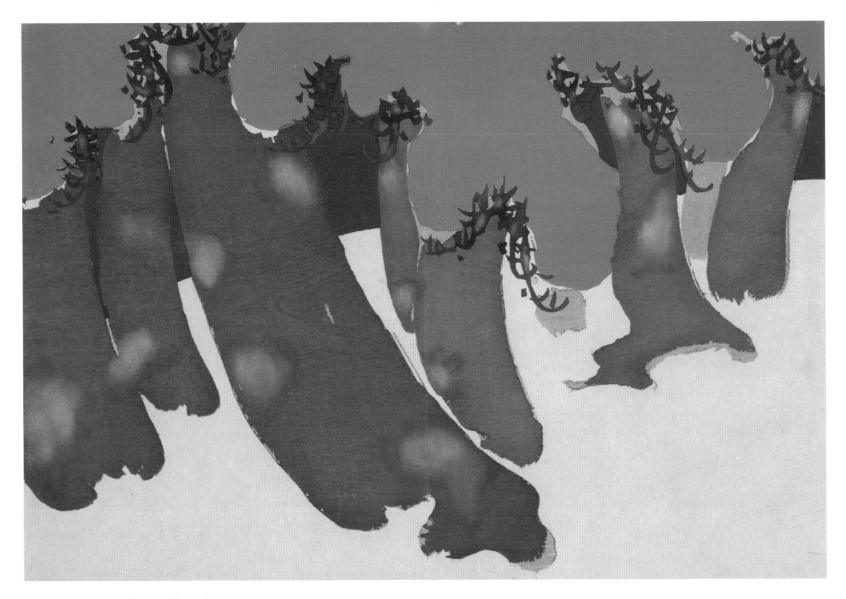

Pine Trees on the Seashore | Sonare no matsu

View of Yoshino | Yoshino

Idleness | Tsurezure

Flower Boat | Hanabune

Late Autumn | Boshū

Nakakuni ("The Tale of the Heike") | Nakakuni

A River in Winter | Fuyu no kawa

The Seven Spring Herbs | Nanakusa

BIBLIOGRAPHY

Fischer, Felice, Edwin A. Cranston, Fumiko E. Cranston, Kyoko Kinoshita, Kumakura Isao, Saito Takamasa, and Yamazaki Tsuyoshi. *The Arts of Hon'ami Kōetsu: Japanese Renaissance Master*. Philadelphia: Philadelphia Museum of Art, 2000.

Hillier, Jack R. *The Art of the Japanese Book*. 2 vols. London: Sotheby's, 1987.

———. "Kamisaka Sekka: Modern Rimpa in Printed Albums." In *Japanese Studies: Papers Presented at a Colloquium at the School of Oriental and African Studies, University of London, 14–16 September, 1988*, edited by Yu-Ying Brown, 219–33. London: British Library, 1990.

Kamisaka Sekka, and Higa Akiko. *Momoyogusa*. Tokyo: Unsōdō, 2003.

Kamisaka Sekka, and Matsubara Ryūichi. *Chō senshu, Kairo*. Tokyo: Unsōdō, 2003.

Kanzaka, Sekka. *A Flight of Butterflies*. New York: Metropolitan Museum of Art, 1979.

Keyes, Roger S. *Ehon: The Artist and the Book in Japan*. New York: New York Public Library, 2006.

Link, Howard. *Exquisite Visions: Rimpa Paintings from Japan*. Honolulu: Honolulu Academy of Arts, 1980.

Machida Shiritsu Kokusai Hanga Bijutsukan [Machida City Museum of Graphic Arts], ed. *Rinpa: Han to kata no tenkai* [Rimpa: splendor of prints and designs]. Machida: Machida City Museum of Graphic Arts, 1992.

Marks, Andreas. *Publishers of Japanese Woodblock Prints: A Compendium*. Leiden, the Netherlands: Brill, Hotei Publishing, 2011.

Sakakibara Yoshirō. *Kamisaka Sekka: Kindai no Rinpa*. Kyoto: Kyōto Shoin, 1981.

Sapin, Julia. "Merchandising Art and Identity in Meiji Japan: Kyoto Nihonga Artists' Designs for Takashimaya Department Store, 1868–1912." *Journal of Design History* 17, no. 4 (2004): 317–36.

Saunders, Rachel. *Le Japon Artistique: Japanese Floral Pattern Design in the Art Nouveau Era from the Collection of the Museum of Fine Arts, Boston*. San Francisco: Chronicle Books, 2010.

Schenk, Sabine. *Zuan: Expressions of Modern Design in Early 20th Century Japanese Art*. Edited by Andreas Marks. Hanford, CA: Clark Center for Japanese Art and Culture, 2010.

Seo, Audrey Y. "Kamisaka Sekka: Master of Japanese Design." *Orientations* 24, no. 12 (1993): 38–44.

Tokubetsu ten Rin-pa: Bi no keishō: Sōtatsu, Kōrin, Hōitsu, Kiitsu. Nagoya: Nagoya City Museum; Chōnichi Shinbun; Chubu Nippon Broadcasting Co., Ltd., 1994.

Wilson, Richard L. *The Art of Ogata Kenzan: Persona and Production in Japanese Ceramics*. New York: Weatherhill, 1991.

Wood, Donald A., and Ikeda Yuko, eds. *Kamisaka Sekka: Rimpa Master—Pioneer of Modern Design*. Kyoto: National Museum of Modern Art, Kyoto; Birmingham, Alabama: Birmingham Museum of Art; Tokyo: Asahi Shimbun, 2003.

Yokoya Kenichirō, and Matsuo Mikio. *Zuanchō in Kyoto: Textile Design Books for the Kimono Trade*. Palo Alto, CA: Stanford University Libraries, 2008.